INSIDE IGLOOS

Written by Amanda Li
Illustrated by Max Rambaldi

Contents

OXFORD
UNIVERSITY PRESS

Words to look out for ...

complicate *VERB*

To complicate something is to make it difficult or awkward.

inspiration *NOUN*

If someone or something is an inspiration, or gives you inspiration, they encourage you or fill you with ideas.

involve *VERB*

To involve something is to need it or result in it.

practical *ADJECTIVE*

Something is practical when it is likely to be useful.

purpose *NOUN*

the reason why you do something; what something is for

respond *VERB*

To respond to someone or something is to reply or react to them.

A shelter of snow

Igloos are amazing buildings made from snow. People believe they are among the oldest kinds of building on Earth.

Imagine that you are somewhere very chilly and everything is covered in snow. Building a house from snow would be a clever and practical way of surviving the cold!

Something is practical when it is likely to be useful.

The frozen north

Igloos are useful in the **Arctic**. The Arctic is one of the coldest places on Earth.

Some of the people who live in the Arctic are called the Inuit. The Inuit once lived in igloos. Now they sometimes build them for **shelter** while out hunting.

an Inuit village

a hunting igloo

Building an igloo!

Building an Inuit igloo <u>involves</u> a lot of hard work.
Let's find out how they are built.

An igloo-builder needs:

- gloves
- a snow shovel
- a snow saw and knife
- hard snow.

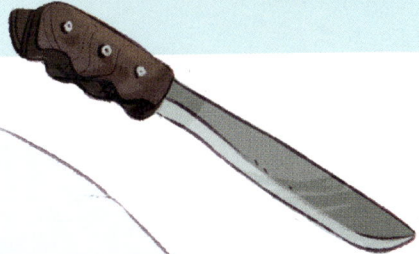

Did you know...

'Iglu' is a word that some
Inuit use to mean 'house'.

To <u>involve</u> something is to need it or result in it.

1

Mark a circle in the snow. For a small igloo, make it about three metres wide.

2

Cut large blocks from hard snow.

3

Stand inside the circle. Fit the blocks together around the edge.

Did you know ...

There are different kinds of snow. Hard, dry, crunchy snow is essential for igloos. Soft, fresh snow cannot be cut into blocks.

4

Build upwards.
Make the circle smaller as you go.

5

As the sides get higher, lean them
inwards to make a **dome** shape.

6

Cut out a small doorway. For extra warmth, dig down and make a tunnel entrance.

7

Put the final blocks in the ceiling. They must fit very tightly or the igloo could collapse!

The big question

Igloos keep people warm, but how can an igloo be warmer inside than outside?

It's all about the snow! Fresh, fluffy snow has lots of air pockets between its snowflakes.

air pockets

In fact, a pile of snow is mostly trapped air. This means it makes fantastic **insulation**.

Heat from your body warms the air inside the igloo. The air stays warm because the snow walls stop the heat escaping. Your body acts like a **stove**.

The more people that are inside, the warmer the igloo will be!

Come on in!

Crawl in and you won't feel the freezing winds outside. The tiny entrance and thick walls keep the cold out.

fire

You could even build a fire! If any snow in the walls melts, the cold air outside re-freezes it.

raised bed

Smoke leaves through a hole in the roof.

Feeling sleepy? Lie down on a 'snow bed' raised above the floor.

It is a warmer place to rest. This is because warm air always rises, and colder air sinks down to the floor.

Strong domes

What do you notice about the shape of all the igloos in this book?

They are all curved!

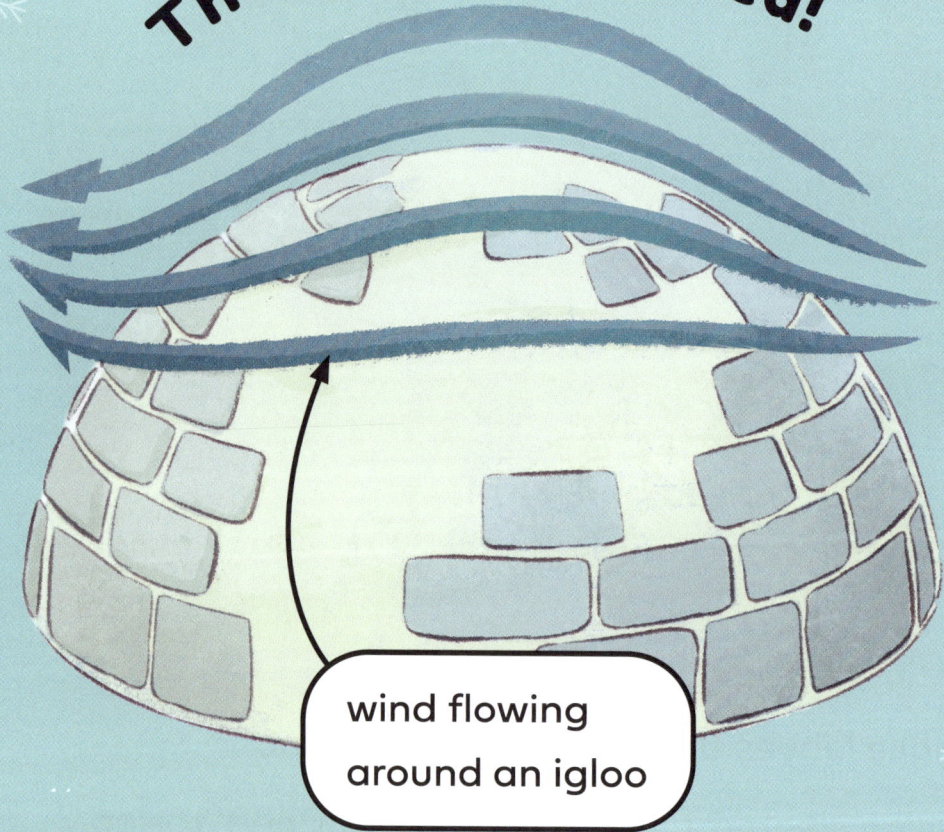

wind flowing around an igloo

This shape is a dome. Domes are incredibly strong. They can stand up against Arctic storms without being blown away.

Domes have been used in buildings for thousands of years. They can hold up their own weight. Their ceilings don't need extra support.

Domes are strong and **stable**. That's why some people are responding to the threat of extreme weather and **earthquakes** by building 'dome homes'.

To respond to someone or something is to reply or react to them.

The freezing Arctic

- About 4 000 000 people live in the Arctic.

- Polar bears, foxes, seals and other wildlife live there too.

- During winter, the surface of the Arctic Ocean freezes into huge sheets of ice.

The Arctic winter is extremely cold. The Inuit dress in practical clothes to keep warm and to avoid dangers like frostbite (when skin begins to freeze).

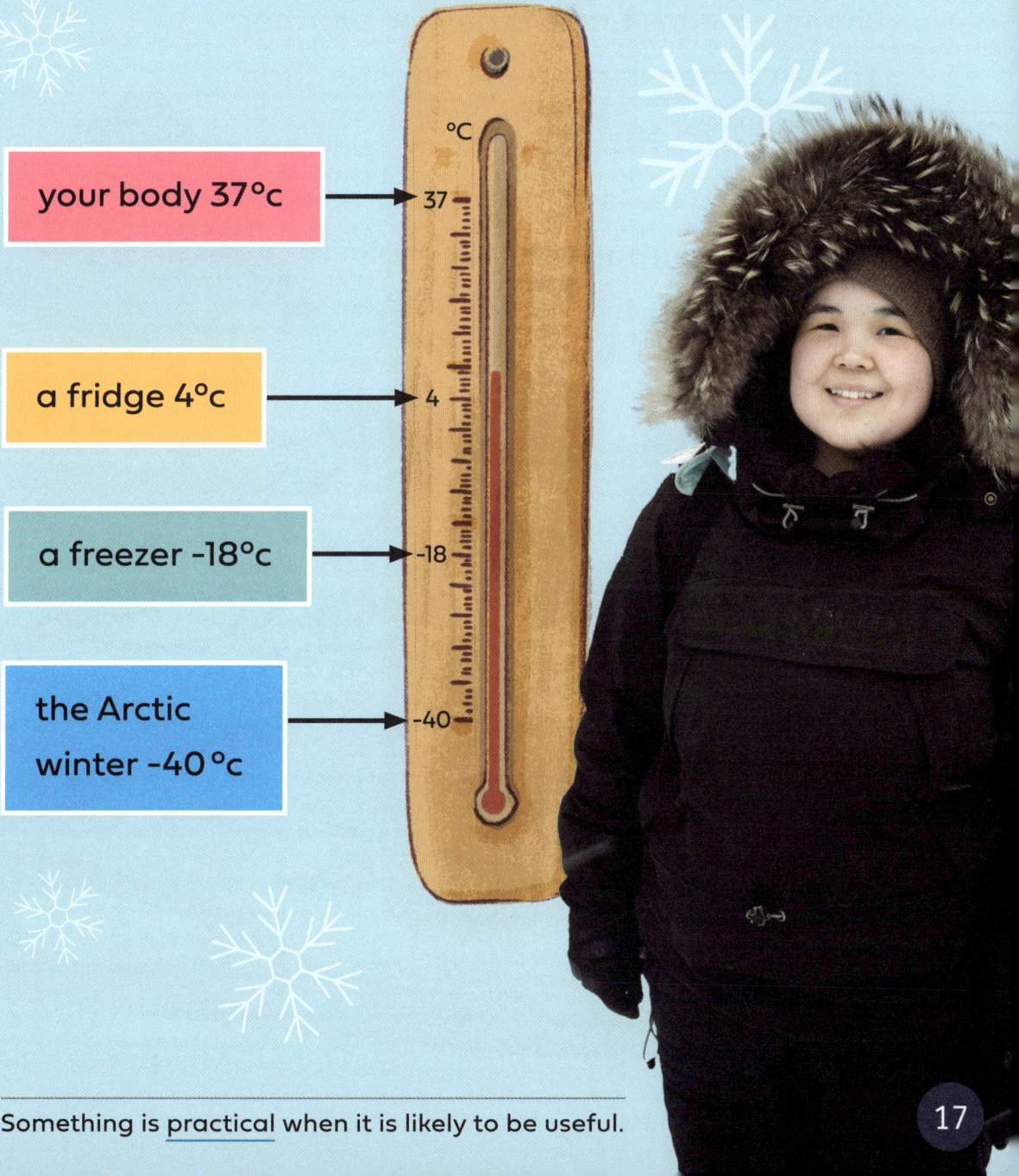

°C

your body 37°c → 37

a fridge 4°c → 4

a freezer -18°c → -18

the Arctic winter -40°c → -40

Something is practical when it is likely to be useful.

The big melt

Everything is changing in the Arctic. **Climate change** means Earth is getting warmer. The Arctic sea ice is melting faster than we have ever seen before.

The melting ice is complicating the lives of humans and animals in the Arctic.

To complicate something is to make it difficult or awkward.

Climate change is having a big impact on the Inuits' way of life. It is harder to travel across the shrinking ice. It is more difficult to hunt for food.

Inuit **activists** of all ages are telling the world about what is happening.

The Inuit activist Maatalii Okalik has talked to leaders around the world about climate change.

Everyday survival

Igloos are perfect for their purpose: for shelter and keeping warm in the freezing cold.

All over the world, people respond to their surroundings in different ways. They use what is around them to create their homes. The homes suit the place.

A purpose is the reason why you do something, or what something is for. To respond to someone or something is to reply or react to them.

In very hot areas, people have lived in cave homes for thousands of years. Cave walls can stop and trap heat from the sun. This means the caves stay cooler in summer.

In places that flood, houses can be built on **stilts**. They are built using bamboo and wood from nearby forests.

It's 'snow' big

How about a cup of hot chocolate in a snow cafe?

The 'Snoglu' is a huge igloo cafe that was built near a ski slope. It may be the biggest igloo ever built!

Did you know...

Snoglu's igloo was eleven metres high and building it involved 7000 snow blocks.

To involve something is to need it or result in it.

An 'ice' place to stay!

Some amazing ice hotels have used igloos as their inspiration. They are built from blocks of snow and ice.

Would you like to sleep on an ice bed?

Whether it's large or small, building an igloo is a fantastic way to stay warm!

If someone or something is an inspiration, or gives you inspiration, they encourage you or fill you with ideas.

Glossary

activists: people who work to change the world around them and inspire others to do the same

Arctic: a snowy region at the very north of Earth

climate change: a change in weather patterns over a long time

dome: a roof shaped like the top half of a ball

earthquakes: when the ground shakes due to rocks moving deep underground

insulation: materials that stop or slow down heat

shelter: protection from the weather and from harm

stable: steady and fixed in place

stilts: sticks that lift something up above the ground

stove: an object that gives out heat for warming a room or for cooking

Index